That was now.

A mindful journal

By Emma Clarke

A Sit. Breathe. Love. Paperback

Sit. Breathe. Love. is an imprint of Identity Withheld Ltd.

First printed in Great Britain in 2014

By Identity Withheld Ltd.

This paperback edition published in 2014

By Identity Withheld Ltd.

Copyright © Emma Clarke 2014

The right of Emma Clarke to be identified as the author of this work has been asserted by her in accordance with the Copyright, Design and Patents Act 1988.

All rights reserved. No part of this publication may be reproduced, stored in a retrieval system, or transmitted, in any form or by any means, electronic, mechanical, photocopying, recording or otherwise, without the prior consent of the copyright owner.

ISBN 978-1-910306-02-4

Typeset by Rebecca Perry at Rebecca Perry Design.

Identity Withheld's policy is to use papers that are natural, renewable and recyclable products and made from wood grown in sustainable forests. The logging and manufacturing processes are expected to conform to the environmental regulations of the country of origin.

www.sitbreathelove.com

www.identitywithheld.com

For Dave

That's you, that is.

Mindfulness mʌIn(d)f(ʊ)lnəs

"Mindfulness can be cultivated by paying attention in a specific way, that is in the present moment, and as non-reactively, non-judgmentally and open-heartedly as possible."

Dr Jon Kabat-Zinn

What is mindfulness?

The present moment is the moment you have now; ultimately, it's the only moment you ever have. As soon as you've recognized 'the present' it's become the past because the moment you thought was 'now' has just passed into the past. The future isn't here yet and the past has just happened, so really all we can ever have is now, this present moment.

The present moment can only be recognized fleetingly before it slips into the past. This journal guides you to seize each moment and be fully present in every moment of your life.

Mindfulness means paying deliberate attention to the present moment, with qualities like compassion, acceptance, patience, kindness and curiosity.

Mindfulness is a way of being that has the potential to change the way you look at the world and all the elements of your life: your work, your relationships, your finances, your playtime – everything. By practicing mindfulness you can make the present moment a more wonderful place to be. And the more you practice, the parts of your life you find challenging and difficult will become easier.

It's been said that mindfulness is awareness of the moment 'from the heart.' This means mindfulness practice gives rise to a deep connection from your inner, most true self to the present moment.

It's true that if you change the way you look at things, the things you look at change. And if it's true that what we resist persists, it's also true that what we accept transforms.

This journal gives you an opportunity to transform the way you perceive your life. Be kind to yourself and try not to judge or criticize what you write, draw, scribble or glue in these pages.

As you embark upon your mindful journey, be prepared to become your true self, fulfilling all your potential and living your life to its absolute fullest.

How to use this journal

This journal helps you live every moment to the max. Each page encourages you to think about your daily experiences in a whole new way, focusing your attention on specific thoughts and senses.

- You'll write an affirmation on every page, to encourage positive thinking.

- You'll think about all the people, situations and stuff you're grateful for, but probably don't notice most of the time.

- You'll tune in to what each of your senses is experiencing, one by one. In this way, you'll connect with your body and the moments of pleasure your body enjoys.

- You'll consider how you spend your time, how you think and feel. How you live your life.

When you follow these simple steps in mindfulness, you'll notice patterns in your thinking. Some of your patterns will be helpful, some perhaps less so. By noticing these patterns, you'll have an opportunity to change them... if that's what you choose to do. And this change could be powerful. Potentially life-changing.

It's your moment. Now.

Ah, that was now.

No, no – THIS is now. This moment.

Er... but that moment's just gone... hasn't it?

DATE ⌊_____/_____/_____⌋

affirmation

intent

Date You can write the date here, or if you fancy it develop a highly sophisticated colour-code system. It's completely up to you.

Affirmation This is a true, personal, positive statement written in the present tense. It's a declaration that this is a fact. For more info on affirmations, check out page 29.

Intent This is an aim, a purpose you have for a day, a month, a year, a moment.

Gratitude This is the attitude you have to things you're thankful for. For more on gratitude, have a read of page 27.

Seeing Everything your eyes (or even your mind's eye) sees: glorious views, light, shadows, faces, colour, horrors, outstanding beauty. This is all about how your visual sense perceives the world.

Hearing Everything you hear: music, talking, whispers, the sounds of nature, laughing. How has what you've heard affected you?

Smelling Everything you smell: food, perfume, detergent, your bed, and even unavoidable terrible smells. Smells can affect our thinking and can evoke memories of specific places, people, moments from your past.

Touching Everything you touch: clothes, surfaces, gorgeous textures, fur, hair, rocks, the skin of someone you love. How have the things you've touched connected you to the world, your thoughts and feelings?

Tasting Everything you've ingested: food, drink, drugs... other substances that have passed your lips and affected your taste sensation.

Thoughts Thoughts aren't facts and the untame tiger of our mind can pull us in all sorts of directions we'd rather not go. How do your thoughts affect your enjoyment?

Feelings Noting down how you feel will show you the pattern your mind prefers to follow, either through habit, conditioning or by restricting your life with fear.

Blank icon This icon might be about food, sex, relationships, exercise, work, money, pets, children, technology – whatever is relevant to you.

Space to write, draw, scribble...

There's really no right or wrong way to fill in your mindfulness journal. Just take your time and enjoy the experience.

How to cultivate mindfulness

By adopting the seven mindsets described below, you can help your mindfulness practice become a way of being. Regular meditation practice is extremely helpful in developing a mindful attitude, but it's not the only way. To cultivate an attitude of compassionate curiosity towards yourself take time to just contemplate, every day, This could be doing star jumps, in deliberate meditation, making a cup of tea, walking, eating your lunch (it could be anything you like). Create a mental space where you limit your distractions and focus on your activity.

1. Non-judging

Take the position of an impartial witness to your own experiences. Become aware of your judgemental thoughts (towards either yourself or others) and take a step back. Notice when you slip into categorizing people and events into 'good' and 'bad', 'positive' and 'negative.' Try to experience them just as they are, without judgements. Notice how often you become preoccupied with 'liking' or 'disliking' something.

2. Patience

Sometimes things unfold in their own time; you don't get daffodils in December! Practicing mindfulness helps us to experience our own unfolding moment by moment. Why rush on to the next moment when we can experience our life in the one we have now?

3. Beginner's mind

Practicing mindfulness means taking the chance to see everything as if we were seeing it for the very first time. Sometimes the illusion of 'knowing' can prevent us from experiencing our lives now in the present, as they really are and not how we expect them to be. Try to see something new in people, places, situations that are very familiar. You might experience them in a new, fresh way.

4. Trust

Trusting yourself is a key part of meditation practice. If you can cultivate a calm and peaceful mind to the point where you can honestly trust yourself you can become wholly and truly yourself.

5. Non-striving

Mindfulness and meditation is really about non-doing; it has no goal other than 'being.' If you meditate and practice mindfulness to get relaxed, stress-free, happy and enlightened you'll struggle to succeed. Just let your practice be what it is, experience every moment for what it is and take what you can from every meditation session.

6. Acceptance

Often acceptance comes after we've been through an intense period of stress or turmoil. Sometimes we can't change things but accepting our circumstances means we stop struggling against them, wasting time and energy on thinking about situations that are beyond our control.

7. Letting go

When we pay attention to our inner experience, we discover there are certain thoughts, feelings and situations that our mind wants to hold on to. If it's a pleasant experience, we try and prolong our pleasure; if it's unpleasant we can either dwell on the source of our discomfort or try to forcefully push it away. In meditation, we try to intentionally put aside our tendency to cling onto some aspects of our experience and reject others.

Obstacles to mindfulness

1. Mindfulness takes ongoing effort.

It's true that daily meditation and mindfulness practice takes effort but the good news is that the more commitment you have to your practice, the greater the benefits you'll experience. You might find that your mind is chaotic, undisciplined and hard to 'pin down' – this is absolutely normal and shows how difficult it can be to train our mind to become peaceful. Focus on being mindful of your thoughts when you're doing everyday tasks and it will be easier to remain mindful when the going gets tough.

2. There will always be distractions.

There will always be really good reasons why you shouldn't meditate: the washing needs doing, you want to watch your favourite TV show, someone is demanding your time. The dramas of our lives can make it hard to find time to meditate. Negative beliefs from your past might clutter your mind and convince you that meditation is a waste of time. Noise might distract you and throw off your concentration. There's no quick route to mindfulness but gently putting aside distractions and focusing on your practice will help you realize who you are.

3. Progress doesn't always come quickly.

Progress might seem excruciatingly slow. You might want proof that you're 'doing it right.' You'll have meditation sessions where you just can't seem to focus your mind. It's impossible to be mindful when you're dwelling on the past or obsessing about the future. Once you start to live in the moment with gratitude, progress will start to happen naturally.

4. You may want to give up.

You might want to throw in the towel and give up many, many times. But it's during the times when you feel most frustrated and blocked that you may be on the verge of a breakthrough. Our lives are like the seasons, like weather – everything passes.

It's the ebb and flow of life. The times when you're full of doubt will pass too. Challenging times help you grow and once you experience this as a realization you'll start to feel more peaceful and relaxed.

5. Your goals may challenge your mindfulness.

Having goals can be helpful but it's easy to become too attached to them and focus purely on the goals themselves and not the practice. You know you're attached to something if you feel frustrated, angry and upset when things don't work out quite how you want them to.

6. You might forget that the journey is the destination.

The reward of mindfulness is the journey itself. With mindfulness, there's actually nowhere really to arrive at. It is in the journey that we learn, grow and become more truthful expressions of ourselves. We often feel we need goals to give us a sense of purpose and fulfilment. Once we let go of this goal-centric, competitive attitude – even if we're only competing against ourselves – and trust in the process of our practice, we can live moment by moment focusing on our practice and not just clocking up the number of minutes we spend in meditation.

7. Sometimes you'll want to be anywhere but in the now.

Life can be painful, frightening and full of uncertainty. Our natural instinct is to shut out painful feelings and experiences; but if we trust ourselves to let go of negative feelings we become the guardians of our own inner space. Letting go of pain is the only way to feel good inside and find peace of mind, right now.

Some questions before you start your journal

Being clear about why you're embarking on a mindfulness journal might help you from the get-go.

So why do I want to start a mindfulness journal?

What do I want to accomplish?

Where I am right now

Defining how you feel now will start your mindfulness practice and help you tune in to the present moment and experience it as fully as you can. Understanding where you are now will help you throughout your mindfulness journey.

How do I feel right now?

If it helps, draw, scribble, doodle or glue stuff HERE.

What does happiness mean for me right now?

Right now, what does peace mean for me?

Who I am

Fill this space with pics, doodles, words (whatever you want) that describe who you are.

My core values are:

My time

By thinking about how you're spending your time you can make mindful choices about the activities that fill your life. Once you've pondered this for a while, you can work out if your current choices are helping you develop a calm, peaceful mind... and if they're not, perhaps you can guide yourself to make a different set of choices that will serve you better.

How I currently spend my time...

How I want to spend my time...

Meditation

There are many different ways to meditate, and as it's such a personal practice there are probably a million different ways to do it. Mindful meditation is where you focus on one specific thing – it could be your breathing, a physical sensation or a particular object outside of you. The purpose of this type of meditation is to focus strongly on one thing and continually and gently bring your attention back to that focus when your mind wanders. (The key word there is 'gently.' If your mind wanders, just gently, super-gently refocus).

It's true that focused attention is very much like a muscle; it needs to be strengthened through exercise. And the more we meditate, the less anxiety we have. This is because we're actually loosening the connections of particular neural pathways.

There's a section of our brain that's sometimes referred to as the Me Centre (it's technically the medial prefrontal cortex). This is the part that processes information relating to ourselves and our experiences, so everything to do with the 'me' part of ourselves. Normally the neural pathways from the bodily sensation and fear centres of the brain to the Me Centre are really strong. **When you experience a scary or upsetting sensation, it triggers a strong reaction in your Me Centre, making you feel scared and under attack.**

When we meditate, we weaken this neural connection. This means that we don't react as strongly to sensations that might have once lit up our Me Centres. As we weaken this connection, we simultaneously strengthen the connection between what's known as our Assessment Centre (the part of our brains known for reasoning) and our bodily sensation and fear centres. **So when we experience scary or upsetting sensations, we can more easily look at them rationally and with much less anxiety.**

For example, when you experience pain, rather than becoming anxious and assuming it means something is wrong with you,

you can watch the pain rise and fall without becoming ensnared in a story about what it might mean.

Scientists have shown that regular meditation can foster more creativity, greater compassion, better memory, less stress and more grey matter.

So meditating is definitely good for you. But how do you do it?

Mindful breathing exercises

Breathing in is such a simple practice but it can transform your life. We all breathe and most of the time, we're not even aware of it. With mindful breathing, when you breathe in, know that you're breathing in. When you breathe out, know you're breathing out. Recognise your breathing; notice it. The great meditation master Thich Nhat Hanh teaches five simple mindfulness exercises to help you live with happiness and joy.

Mindfulness practice should be enjoyable, and shouldn't take great effort. Breathing in doesn't take much effort and we don't often think about it – we just do it. To breathe in, just breathe in. Simply allow your breath to take place. As you do it, become aware of it and enjoy it, all of it, effortlessly.

The same thing is true with walking mindfully. We walk a lot. We don't often think about it. With mindful walking, every step you take is enjoyable. Every step helps you become aware of the wonders of life, in yourself and around you. Every step is a step towards inner peace. Every step is connecting with the earth. Every step is an opportunity to feel joy.

During the time you are practicing mindfulness, you stop talking – not only the talking outside, but the talking inside that constantly goes on in our heads. This internal dialogue goes on and on and on inside you, without you really being conscious of the quality of thoughts that flit across your mind. Real silence is the cessation of talking – of both the mouth and of the mind. This silence isn't oppressive or restrictive. It's a very elegant, powerful kind of silence. It is the kind of silence that heals and nourishes us.

Another source of happiness is concentration. When you are aware of something, such as breathing, walking or even a blade of grass, and can maintain that awareness, your focus is concentrated. When your mindfulness becomes powerful, your concentration becomes powerful, and when you are fully concentrated, you have a chance to make a breakthrough and achieve insight. If you meditate on a cloud, you can get insight into the nature of the cloud. You can meditate on yourself, or negative feelings like anger and fear, or your sense of joy and peace.

Anything can be the object of your meditation – people, places, objects, food, music, art – and with the powerful energy of concentration, you can make a breakthrough and develop insight. When your mindfulness and concentration are powerful, your insight will liberate you from fear, anger, and despair, and bring you true joy, true peace, and true happiness.

Mindful breathing

The first exercise is very simple, but the results can be transformative. The exercise is simply to identify the in-breath as in-breath and the out-breath as the out-breath. When you breathe in, you know that this is your in-breath. When you breathe out, you are mindful that this is your out-breath.

Just recognize: this is an in-breath, this is an out-breath. It really is that simple. In order to recognize your in-breath as in-breath, you have to bring your mind gently 'home' to yourself and your breathing. The object of your mindfulness is your breath, and you just focus your attention on it. Breathing in, this is your in-breath. Breathing out, this is your out-breath. When you do that, the mental chatter will stop. You don't think or follow your own internal dialogue any more. You don't have to make an effort to stop your thinking; you bring your attention to your in-breath and the mental chatter just stops. You don't think of the past any more. You don't think of the future. You just focus your attention, your mindfulness, on your breath.

You are breathing in, and while breathing in, you know that you are alive. The in-breath can be a celebration of the fact that you are alive, so it can be very joyful. When you are joyful and happy, you don't feel that you have to make any effort at all. You are alive; you are breathing in. To be still alive is a miracle. The greatest of all miracles is to be alive, and when you breathe in, you touch that miracle. In this way, you can experience your breathing as a celebration of life.

An in-breath may take three, four, five seconds, maybe more. That's time to be alive, time to enjoy your breath. You don't have to interfere with your breathing. If your in-breath is short, allow it to be short. If your out-breath is long, let it to be long. Don't try to force it. The practice is simple recognition of the in-breath and the out-breath.

Concentration

The second exercise is about concentration – that while you breathe in, you follow your in-breath from the beginning to the end. If your in-breath lasts three or four seconds, then your mindfulness also lasts three or four seconds. From the beginning of your out-breath to the end of your out-breath, your mind is always with it. Therefore, mindfulness becomes uninterrupted, and the quality of your concentration is improved.

So the second exercise is to follow your in-breath and your out-breath all the way through. Whether they are short or long, it doesn't matter. What is important is that you follow your in-breath from the very beginning to the very end. Your awareness is sustained with no interruption. Suppose you are breathing in, and then you think, "Oh, I forgot to send an email." There is an interruption. Just stick to your in-breath all the way through. Then you cultivate your mindfulness and your concentration. You become your in-breath. You become your out-breath. If you continue like that, your breathing will naturally become deeper and slower, more harmonious and peaceful. You don't have to make any effort – it just happens naturally.

Awareness of your body

The third exercise is to become aware of your body as you are breathing. "Breathing in, I am aware of my whole body." This takes the practice one step further.

In the first exercise, you became aware of your in-breath and your out-breath. Because you have now generated the energy of mindfulness through mindful breathing, you can use that energy to recognize your body.

"Breathing in, I am aware of my body. Breathing out, I am aware of my body." When your mind is with your body, you are well-established in the here and the now. You know your body is there. You are fully alive. You can be in touch with the wonders of life that are available in yourself and around you.

This exercise is simple, but the effect of the oneness of body and mind is very great. In our daily lives, we are rarely in that situation. Our body is there but our mind is elsewhere. Our mind gets caught in the past or in the future, in regrets, sorrow, fear, or uncertainty, and so our mind is not present. Our mind could be off with the future, with our projects, and we're not there for our children or our partner.

When you practice mindful breathing, there is more peace and harmony in your breathing, and if you continue this practice, the peace and the harmony will penetrates into your body, into your being.

Releasing tension

The next exercise is to release the tension in the body. When you are truly aware of your body, you notice there is some tension and pain in your body, some kind of stress. The tension and pain might have been accumulating for a long time and our bodies suffer. We often don't realise how physically tense we are until we focus our minds on noticing it.

It doesn't matter what position you're in – sitting, lying, or standing – it's always possible to release the tension. You can practice total relaxation, deep relaxation, in a sitting or lying position.

While you are driving, you might notice the tension in your body, a stiffness in your jaw, neck and shoulders. You are in a hurry and feel stressed about the traffic. When you come to a red light, you're impatient to get moving again. But the red light can be a reminder to try and relax. Take opportunity offered by the red light to practice mindful breathing and release the tension in the body.

So next time you're stopped at a red light, you might like to sit back and practice the fourth exercise: "Breathing in, I'm aware of my body. Breathing out, I release the tension in my body." Peace is possible at that moment, and it can be practiced many times a day – at work, while you are driving, while you are cooking, while you are doing the dishes, while you are walking. It is always possible to practice releasing the tension in your body; it follows that when you do that, the tension in your mind eases at the same time.

Walking meditation

When you practice mindful breathing you simply allow your in-breath to take place. You become aware of it and enjoy it without effort. The same thing is true with mindful walking. Every step is enjoyable. Every step helps you touch the wonders of life. Every step has the potential for great joy.

You don't have to make any effort during walking meditation, because it is so simple, so enjoyable. You are there, body and mind together. You are fully alive, fully present in the here and the now. With every step, you can celebrate the wonder of life and appreciate everything that is around you. When you walk mindfully, every step brings healing. Every step brings peace and joy, because every step is a miracle.

The real miracle is not to fly or walk on fire. The real miracle is to walk on the Earth, and you can perform that miracle at any time. Just bring your mind home to your body, become alive, and perform the joyful miracle of walking on Earth.

To learn more about Thich Nhat Hanh and teachings, we recommend his book 'The Miracle of Mindfulness.'

Gratitude

Gratitude is an emotion that expresses appreciation for what we have – as opposed to a consumer-oriented emphasis on what we (think we) want or need. Gratitude is what gets poured into the metaphorical glass to make it half full. Studies show that gratitude not only can be deliberately cultivated but can increase levels of well-being and happiness among those try to cultivate it. In addition, grateful thinking – and especially expression of it to others – is associated with increased levels of energy, optimism, and empathy.

With this in mind, here's a list of 'gratitude questions' that might help you develop a more grateful attitude to your life.

1. Who do I appreciate?
2. How am I fortunate?
3. What material possessions am I grateful for?
4. What abilities do I have that I'm grateful for?
5. What about my surroundings am I grateful for?
6. What experience have I had that I'm grateful for?
7. What happened this week that I'm grateful for?
8. What opportunities do I have that I'm grateful for?
9. What have others done in my life that I'm grateful for?
10. What have others done that I'm benefiting from in my life?
11. What relationships am I thankful for?
12. What am I taking for granted?

13. What is there about the challenges and difficulties I have experienced that I'm grateful for?
14. What is different today than it was a year ago that I'm grateful for?
15. What insights have I gained that I'm grateful for?
16. What am I able to offer others that I'm grateful for?
17. What opportunities to help others am I grateful for?
18. What changes have happened that I'm grateful for?
19. What can I find to be grateful for this very moment?
20. What can I enjoy right now that I can be grateful for?
21. What have I learned lately that I'm grateful for?
22. Who am I grateful for, for teaching me something today?
23. What do I get to do that I'm grateful for?
24. What physical sensation am I grateful for right now?
25. What object am I most grateful for?
26. What physical attribute am I most grateful for?
27. What advice am I most grateful for?
28. Which mentor am I most thankful for?
29. Which memory am I most grateful for?
30. What is the subtlest thing I can notice and be grateful for?

There's space on every journal page for you to focus on something you realise you feel specifically grateful for as your filling in your entry.

Affirmations

Developing your own set of affirmations will help you develop positive thinking and a sense of self-empowerment. An affirmation is a carefully worded statement that should be repeated to yourself often and written down. For an affirmation to be effective, it needs to be present tense, positive, personal and specific.

Here are some examples:

1. I am the architect of my life. I build its foundations and choose its contents.

2. Today I am brimming with energy and overflowing with joy.

3. My energy is vibrant; my mind is brilliant; my soul is tranquil.

4. I am superior to negative thoughts and low actions.

5. I have been given endless talents that I will utilize today.

6. I forgive those who have harmed me in my past and I peacefully detach from them.

7. A river of compassion washes away my anger and replaces it with love.

8. My relationships become stronger, deeper and more stable every day.

9. I take pleasure in my own solitude.

10. I trust myself.

There's space in your every journal entry for you to write down an affirmation.

Some mindfulness exercises

1. Look at a picture. Note down everything you notice about it. The light, the objects, the people – everything.

2. Spend some time watching the sky. Draw what you see, or write a commentary about how it changes.

3. Notice how nature is changing now we're moving into a new season. What do you notice? Look deeply and use all your senses.

4. Experience the weather. Whatever the weather, really feel how your body responds to your environment. How do you feel physically? Emotionally? Write about how you feel, or draw a picture.

5. Explore a place you're familiar with, with your eyes closed. Use your hands, nose, ears.

6. Take two mindful bites of your favourite food. Notice its texture, taste, smell as you eat it.

7. Spend some time looking at an object from the natural world. Imagine where it came from. How it would feel to touch it.

8. Observe an animal. How would it feel to be that animal? How does the animal feel about its world?

9. Notice the gap or space between your thoughts.

10. Choose a tree. Get to know it. Break its leaves – how does it smell? What sounds does it make? Use your senses.

11. Go outside and feel the air on your skin. It might be windy, it might be warm. Wear short sleeves to get the best experience.

12. Create your own Mindfulness spot. It could be a place outside, inside, wherever you want it to be. But it should be a place that would be good for you to spend a lot of time.

13. Sit in a place that feels good and make a list of everything you observe.

14. Try slow motion walking. Become aware of precisely how your body moves as you take a couple of steps. Go as slowly as you can.

15. Hold a piece of fruit. Use your senses. How did that fruit grow? Imagine you're inside the fruit, as it ripens and gets picked. Feel how the fruit feels in your hand.

16. When you're waiting for something, what do you notice? It could be a train, an appointment, a kettle to boil.

17. When you're in the middle of something, what does your internal process feel like? How does your mind process information?

18. Walk barefoot around your house and in an outside space. Feel the floor and the earth beneath you as you walk; feel connected to your environment.

19. Where are you in your life this moment?

20. List everything you're grateful for today.

21. Imagine your peaceful mind as a beautiful blue sky. As your thoughts pass across your consciousness, visualize them as clouds that drift, shift and move across the sky.

22. Write down this month's successes.

23. How do you eat your lunch?

24. When you do your mindful breathing exercises, imagine you're breathing in cool, blue light. When you breathe out, you exhale hot black smoke that symbolizes all the negative feelings you experience.

25. What do you notice on your journey to work?

26. Try a social media fast.

27. Listen to a piece of music. Try to hear it as though for the first time. Feel the texture of the music, the range of instruments, the rhythm. If the music were transformed into a light show, how would it look?

28. When you return after a holiday, what do you notice about your home. Use your senses.

29. Write about specific memories from last Christmas — tastes, smells, images, phrases, people, places, objects.

30. What experiences, feelings and habits do you want to let go of at the end of the year?

31. Appreciate your hands. Focus on what your hands do for you.

32. Look at your body with loving eyes.

33. What feelings, thoughts and inspiration can you bring to the new year?

34. Look deeply into food. Use the power of imagination to see where it comes from and how many people might have been involved in bringing it to your plate.

35. Go into your kitchen. Choose something to focus on. Look at it, touch it, use it. Write about it.

36. Keep track of your urges (this could be for food, a person, an activity, a place). Look at why you feel this way. What do you hope to feel if you carry out the urge? Is it likely the urge will make you feel better?

Your Journal

DATE ____/____/____

affirmation ....
....

   intent ....
....

Space to write, draw, scribble...

DATE _____/_____/_____

affirmation ....
....

intent ....
....

Space to write, draw, scribble...

DATE ____/_____/_____

affirmation ....
....

   intent ....
....

Space to write, draw, scribble...

DATE ⌊_____/_____/_____⌋

affirmation ....
....

    intent ....
....

Space to write, draw, scribble...

DATE ⌊_____/_____/_____⌋

affirmation ....
....

    intent ....
....

Space to write, draw, scribble...

DATE ____/____/____

affirmation ....

....

intent ....

....

Space to write, draw, scribble...

DATE _____/_____/_____

affirmation ....
....

    intent ....
....

Space to write, draw, scribble...

DATE ___/___/___

affirmation ....
....

intent ....
....

Space to write, draw, scribble...

DATE   /   /

affirmation ....
....

   intent ....
....

Space to write, draw, scribble...

DATE ⌊_____/_____/_____⌋

affirmation ....
....
     intent ....
....

Space to write, draw, scribble...

DATE ⌞_____/_____/_____⌟

affirmation ....
....

    intent ....
....

Space to write, draw, scribble...

DATE ____/____/____

affirmation ....
....

intent ....
....

Space to write, draw, scribble...

DATE ___/___/___

affirmation ....
....

　　　intent ....
....

Space to write, draw, scribble...

DATE ___/___/___

affirmation ....
....

intent ....
....

Space to write, draw, scribble...

DATE ⌊_____/_____/_____⌋

affirmation ....
....

    intent ....
....

Space to write, draw, scribble...

DATE ⌊_____/_____/_____⌋

affirmation ....
....
    intent ....
....

Space to write, draw, scribble...

DATE ⌊_____/_____/_____⌋

affirmation ....
....

   intent ....
....

Space to write, draw, scribble...

DATE ___/___/___

affirmation ....
....

intent ....
....

Space to write, draw, scribble...

DATE ___/___/___

affirmation ....
....

    intent ....
....

Space to write, draw, scribble...

DATE ___/___/___

affirmation ....
....

intent ....
....

Space to write, draw, scribble...

DATE ⌊_____/_____/_____⌋

affirmation ....
....

    intent ....
....

Space to write, draw, scribble...

DATE ____/____/____

affirmation ....
....

intent ....
....

Space to write, draw, scribble...

DATE ____/____/____

affirmation ....
....

　　　intent ....
....

Space to write, draw, scribble...

DATE _____/_____/_____

affirmation ....
....

intent ....
....

Space to write, draw, scribble...

DATE   /   /

affirmation ....
....

    intent ....
....

Space to write, draw, scribble...

DATE ⌊_____/_____/_____⌋

affirmation ....
....

    intent ....
....

Space to write, draw, scribble...

DATE / /

affirmation ....
....

intent ....
....

Space to write, draw, scribble...

DATE ⌊_____/_____/_____⌋

affirmation ....
....

intent ....
....

Space to write, draw, scribble...

DATE ⌊_____/_____/_____⌋

affirmation ....
....

   intent ....
....

Space to write, draw, scribble...

DATE _____ / _____ / _____

affirmation ....
....
    intent ....
....

Space to write, draw, scribble...

DATE _____ / _____ / _____

affirmation ....
....

intent ....
....

Space to write, draw, scribble...

DATE ⌊_____/_____/_____⌋

affirmation ....
....

    intent ....
....

Space to write, draw, scribble...

Checking in

For the next few weeks, I intend to...

What I'm feeling now is...

I am aware that...

I am inspired by...

What motivates me is...

This month, I want to remember...

I wish...

Others are…

What matters most to me now is…

My strengths are…

My weaknesses are…

Things that annoy me are…

I hope that…

Reflecting on the past few weeks

A challenge I tackled recently...

The past few weeks looked like this...

The past few weeks sounded like this...

Last month started like this...

Last month ended like this...

My favourite moment of the past few weeks is...

This month I noticed...

This month I learned...

DATE ..../......./.........

affirmation ....
....

    intent ....
....

Space to write, draw, scribble...

DATE ____/____/____

affirmation ....
....

intent ....
....

Space to write, draw, scribble...

DATE ___/___/___

affirmation ....
....

  intent ....
....

Space to write, draw, scribble...

DATE ____/____/____

affirmation ....
....

   intent ....
....

Space to write, draw, scribble...

DATE ___/___/___

affirmation ....
....

intent ....
....

Space to write, draw, scribble...

DATE _____/_____/_____

affirmation ....
....
    intent ....
....

Space to write, draw, scribble...

DATE _____/_____/_____

affirmation ....
....

   intent ....

Space to write, draw, scribble...

DATE ___/___/___

affirmation ....
....

   intent ....
....

Space to write, draw, scribble...

DATE ⌊_____/_____/_____⌋

affirmation ....
....

   intent ....
....

Space to write, draw, scribble...

DATE ____/____/____

affirmation ....
....

intent ....
....

Space to write, draw, scribble...

DATE ___/___/___

affirmation ....
....

    intent ....
....

Space to write, draw, scribble...

DATE ____/____/____

affirmation ....
....
   intent ....
....

Space to write, draw, scribble...

DATE _____/_____/_____

affirmation ....
....

    intent ....
....

Space to write, draw, scribble...

DATE ____ / ____ / ____

affirmation ....
....
    intent ....
....

Space to write, draw, scribble...

DATE _____/_____/_____

affirmation ....
....

   intent ....
....

Space to write, draw, scribble...

DATE ____/____/____

affirmation ....
....

   intent ....
....

Space to write, draw, scribble...

DATE ____/____/____

affirmation ....
....

   intent ....
....

Space to write, draw, scribble...

DATE ____/____/____

affirmation ....
....

   intent ....
....

Space to write, draw, scribble...

DATE _____/_____/_____

affirmation ....
....

    intent ....
....

Space to write, draw, scribble...

DATE ____/____/____

affirmation ....
....

intent ....
....

Space to write, draw, scribble...

DATE ⌊_____/_____/_____⌋

affirmation ....
....

    intent ....
....

Space to write, draw, scribble...

DATE ___/___/___

affirmation ....
....
   intent ....
....

Space to write, draw, scribble...

DATE ____/____/____

affirmation ....
....

    intent ....
....

Space to write, draw, scribble...

DATE ___/___/___

affirmation ....
....

intent ....
....

Space to write, draw, scribble...

DATE _____/_____/_____

affirmation ....
....

   intent ....
....

Space to write, draw, scribble...

DATE ____/____/____

affirmation ....
....

intent ....
....

Space to write, draw, scribble...

DATE ⌊_____/_____/_____⌋

affirmation ....
....

    intent ....
....

Space to write, draw, scribble...

DATE ____/____/____

affirmation ....
....

intent ....
....

Space to write, draw, scribble...

DATE ____/____/____

affirmation ....
....

    intent ....
....

Space to write, draw, scribble...

DATE _____ / _____ / _____

affirmation ....
....
    intent ....
....

Space to write, draw, scribble...

DATE ____/____/____

affirmation ....
....

   intent ....
....

Space to write, draw, scribble...

DATE _____/_____/_____

affirmation ....
....
   intent ....
....

_____

_____

_____

_____

_____

_____

_____

_____

Space to write, draw, scribble...

Checking in

For the next few weeks, I intend to...

What I'm feeling now is...

I am aware that...

I am inspired by...

What motivates me is...

This month, I want to remember...

I wish...

Others are...

What matters most to me now is...

My strengths are...

My weaknesses are...

Things that annoy me are...

I hope that...

Reflecting on the past few weeks

A challenge I tackled recently...

The past few weeks looked like this...

The past few weeks sounded like this...

Last month started like this...

Last month ended like this...

My favourite moment of the past few weeks is...

This month I noticed...

This month I learned...

DATE ____/____/____

affirmation ....
....

intent ....
....

Space to write, draw, scribble...

DATE ___/___/___

affirmation ....
....

    intent ....
....

Space to write, draw, scribble...

DATE _____ / _____ / _____

affirmation ....
....

   intent ....
....

Space to write, draw, scribble...

DATE ⌊_____/_____/_____⌋

affirmation ....
....
　　intent ....
....

Space to write, draw, scribble...

DATE ___/___/___

affirmation ....
....

   intent ....
....

Space to write, draw, scribble...

DATE   /   /

affirmation ....
....

   intent ....
....

Space to write, draw, scribble...

DATE ___/___/___

affirmation ....

....

intent ....

....

Space to write, draw, scribble...

DATE ____/____/____

affirmation ....
....
   intent ....
....

Space to write, draw, scribble...

DATE ⌊_____ / _____ / _____⌋

affirmation ....
....

    intent ....
....

Space to write, draw, scribble...

DATE ____ / ____ / ____

affirmation ....
....
intent ....
....

Space to write, draw, scribble...

DATE ___/___/_____

affirmation ....
....

    intent ....
....

Space to write, draw, scribble...

DATE ⌊_____/_____/_____⌋

affirmation ....
....

　　intent ....
....

Space to write, draw, scribble...

DATE ⌊_____/_____/_____⌋

affirmation ....
....

    intent ....
....

Space to write, draw, scribble...

DATE ____/____/____

affirmation ....
....

intent ....
....

Space to write, draw, scribble...

DATE ⌊_____/_____/_____⌋

affirmation ....
....

   intent ....
....

Space to write, draw, scribble...

DATE ⌊_____/_____/_____⌋

affirmation ....
....

  intent ....
....

Space to write, draw, scribble...

DATE ⌊_____/_____/_____⌋

affirmation ....
....

      intent ....
....

Space to write, draw, scribble...

DATE ⌊_____/_____/_____⌋

affirmation ....
....

  intent ....
....

Space to write, draw, scribble...

DATE _____/_____/_____

affirmation ....
....

     intent ....
....

Space to write, draw, scribble...

DATE ⌊_____/_____/_____⌋

affirmation ....

....

      intent ....

....

Space to write, draw, scribble...

DATE ⌊_____/_____/_____⌋

affirmation ....
....

   intent ....
....

Space to write, draw, scribble...

DATE ___/___/___

affirmation ....
....

intent ....
....

Space to write, draw, scribble...

DATE ____/____/____

affirmation ....
....

   intent ....
....

Space to write, draw, scribble...

DATE   /   /

affirmation ....
....
       intent ....
....

Space to write, draw, scribble...

DATE ___/___/___

affirmation ....

....

    intent ....

....

Space to write, draw, scribble...

DATE ____ / ____ / ____

affirmation ....
....

intent ....
....

Space to write, draw, scribble...

DATE ⌞_____/_____/_____⌟

affirmation ....
....

      intent ....
....

Space to write, draw, scribble...

DATE ⌊_____/_____/_____⌋

affirmation ....
....

    intent ....
....

Space to write, draw, scribble...

DATE ⌊_____/_____/_____⌋

affirmation ....
....

    intent ....
....

Space to write, draw, scribble...

DATE ┌─────────/─────────/─────────┐

affirmation ....
....
     intent ....
....

Space to write, draw, scribble...

DATE _____/_____/_____

affirmation ....
....

    intent ....
....

Space to write, draw, scribble...

DATE ____/____/____

affirmation ....
....

intent ....
....

Space to write, draw, scribble...

Checking in

For the next few weeks, I intend to…

What I'm feeling now is…

I am aware that…

I am inspired by…

What motivates me is…

This month, I want to remember…

I wish…

Others are...

What matters most to me now is...

My strengths are...

My weaknesses are...

Things that annoy me are...

I hope that...

Reflecting on the past few weeks

A challenge I tackled recently...

The past few weeks looked like this...

The past few weeks sounded like this...

Last month started like this...

Last month ended like this...

My favourite moment of the past few weeks is...

This month I noticed...

This month I learned...

DATE ⌊_____/_____/_____⌋

affirmation ....
....

    intent ....
....

Space to write, draw, scribble...

DATE ___/___/___

affirmation ....
....
    intent ....
....

Space to write, draw, scribble...

DATE ____/____/____

affirmation ....
....

intent ....
....

Space to write, draw, scribble...

DATE ___/___/___

affirmation ....
....

intent ....
....

Space to write, draw, scribble...

DATE ____/____/____

affirmation ....
....

   intent ....
....

Space to write, draw, scribble...

DATE ___/___/___

affirmation ....
....

    intent ....
....

Space to write, draw, scribble...

DATE ⌞_____/_____/_____⌟

affirmation ....
....

intent ....
....

Space to write, draw, scribble...

DATE ⌊_____/_____/_____⌋

affirmation ....
....

    intent ....
....

Space to write, draw, scribble...

DATE ⌊_____/_____/_____⌋

affirmation ....
....

    intent ....
....

Space to write, draw, scribble...

DATE _____/_____/_____

affirmation ....
....

    intent ....
....

🎁	_____
👁	_____
👂	_____
👃	_____
✋	_____
👅	_____
🧠	_____
❤️	_____
☐	

Space to write, draw, scribble...

DATE ___/___/___

affirmation ....
....

intent ....
....

Space to write, draw, scribble...

DATE ____/____/____

affirmation ....
....

intent ....
....

Space to write, draw, scribble...

DATE ..../........../..........

affirmation ....
....

    intent ....
....

Space to write, draw, scribble...

DATE ____/____/____

affirmation ....
....
  intent ....
....

Space to write, draw, scribble...

DATE ___/___/___

affirmation ....
....

intent ....
....

Space to write, draw, scribble...

DATE ____/____/____

affirmation ....
....
   intent ....
....

Space to write, draw, scribble...

DATE ⌊_____/_____/_____⌋

affirmation ....
....

    intent ....
....

Space to write, draw, scribble...

DATE   /   /

affirmation ....
....

   intent ....
....

Space to write, draw, scribble...

DATE ____/____/____

affirmation ....

....

  intent ....

....

Space to write, draw, scribble...

DATE ____/____/____

affirmation ....
....

    intent ....
....

Space to write, draw, scribble...

DATE _____/_____/_____

affirmation ....
....

   intent ....
....

Space to write, draw, scribble...

DATE ___/___/___

affirmation ....
....

intent ....
....

Space to write, draw, scribble...

DATE ⌊_____/_____/_____⌋

affirmation ....
....
    intent ....
....

Space to write, draw, scribble...

DATE ____/____/____

affirmation ....
....
    intent ....
....

Space to write, draw, scribble...

DATE   /   /

affirmation ....
....

    intent ....
....

Space to write, draw, scribble...

DATE ____/____/____

affirmation ....
....
   intent ....
....

Space to write, draw, scribble...

DATE ____ / ____ / ____

affirmation ....
....

   intent ....
....

Space to write, draw, scribble...

DATE ____/____/____

affirmation ....
....
  intent ....
....

Space to write, draw, scribble...

DATE ___/___/___

affirmation ....
....

   intent ....
....

Space to write, draw, scribble...

DATE ⌊_____/_____/_____⌋

affirmation ....
....

   intent ....
....

Space to write, draw, scribble...

DATE ____/____/____

affirmation ....
....

    intent ....
....

Space to write, draw, scribble...

DATE ____/____/____

affirmation ....
....
intent ....
....

Space to write, draw, scribble...

Checking in

For the next few weeks, I intend to...

What I'm feeling now is...

I am aware that...

I am inspired by...

What motivates me is...

This month, I want to remember...

I wish...

Others are...

What matters most to me now is...

My strengths are...

My weaknesses are...

Things that annoy me are...

I hope that...

Reflecting on the past few weeks

A challenge I tackled recently...

The past few weeks looked like this...

The past few weeks sounded like this...

Last month started like this...

Last month ended like this...

My favourite moment of the past few weeks is...

This month I noticed...

This month I learned...

DATE ___/___/___

affirmation ....
....

intent ....
....

Space to write, draw, scribble...

DATE ____/____/____

affirmation ....
....

   intent ....
....

Space to write, draw, scribble...

DATE ___/___/___

affirmation ....
....

intent ....
....

Space to write, draw, scribble...

DATE ____/____/____

affirmation ....
....

intent ....
....

Space to write, draw, scribble...

DATE ⌊_____/_____/_____⌋

affirmation ....
....

  intent ....
....

Space to write, draw, scribble...

DATE ___/___/___

affirmation ....

....

    intent ....

....

Space to write, draw, scribble...

DATE   /   /

affirmation ....
....
        intent ....
....

Space to write, draw, scribble...

DATE _____ / _____ / _____

affirmation ....
....

intent ....
....

Space to write, draw, scribble...

DATE / /

affirmation ....
....

intent ....
....

Space to write, draw, scribble...

DATE ____/____/____

affirmation ....
....
      intent ....
....

Space to write, draw, scribble...

DATE ____/____/____

affirmation ....
....
   intent ....
....

Space to write, draw, scribble...

DATE ⌊_____/_____/_____⌋

affirmation ....
....

intent ....
....

Space to write, draw, scribble...

DATE ____/____/____

affirmation ....
....

intent ....
....

Space to write, draw, scribble...

DATE / /

affirmation ....
....
  intent ....
....

Space to write, draw, scribble...

DATE ⌊⎯⎯⎯⎯⎯⎯/⎯⎯⎯⎯⎯⎯/⎯⎯⎯⎯⎯⎯⌋

affirmation ....
....

   intent ....
....

Space to write, draw, scribble...

DATE ⌊_____/_____/_____⌋

affirmation ....
....
   intent ....
....

Space to write, draw, scribble...

DATE ____/____/____

affirmation ....
....

    intent ....
....

Space to write, draw, scribble...

DATE ___/___/___

affirmation ....
....

intent ....
....

Space to write, draw, scribble...

DATE _____/_____/_____

affirmation ....
....

    intent ....
....

Space to write, draw, scribble...

DATE ___/___/___

affirmation ....
....

intent ....
....

Space to write, draw, scribble...

DATE ____/____/____

affirmation ....
....

   intent ....
....

Space to write, draw, scribble...

DATE ⌊_____/_____/_____⌋

affirmation ....
....
　　　intent ....
....

Space to write, draw, scribble...

DATE ___/___/___

affirmation ....
....

    intent ....
....

Space to write, draw, scribble...

DATE ⌊_____/_____/_____⌋

affirmation ....
....

intent ....
....

Space to write, draw, scribble...

DATE ___/___/___

affirmation ....
....

   intent ....
....

Space to write, draw, scribble...

DATE ⌞_____/_____/_____⌟

affirmation ....
....
   intent ....
....

Space to write, draw, scribble...

DATE / /

affirmation ....
....

intent ....
....

Space to write, draw, scribble...

DATE ⌊_____/_____/_____⌋

affirmation ....
....

    intent ....
....

Space to write, draw, scribble...

DATE _____/_____/_____

affirmation ....
....

   intent ....
....

Space to write, draw, scribble...

DATE _____ / _____ / _____

affirmation ....
....

intent ....
....

Space to write, draw, scribble...

DATE _____/_____/_____

affirmation ....
....

   intent ....
....

Space to write, draw, scribble...

DATE ____ / ____ / ____

affirmation ....
....

    intent ....
....

Space to write, draw, scribble...

Checking in

For the next few weeks, I intend to...

What I'm feeling now is...

I am aware that...

I am inspired by...

What motivates me is...

This month, I want to remember...

I wish...

Others are...

What matters most to me now is...

My strengths are...

My weaknesses are...

Things that annoy me are...

I hope that...

Reflecting on the past few weeks

A challenge I tackled recently...

The past few weeks looked like this...

The past few weeks sounded like this...

Last month started like this...

Last month ended like this...

My favourite moment of the past few weeks is...

This month I noticed...

This month I learned...

DATE ____/____/____

affirmation ....
....

    intent ....
....

Space to write, draw, scribble...

DATE   /   /

affirmation ....
....
    intent ....
....

Space to write, draw, scribble...

DATE ⌐   /   /   ⌐

affirmation ....
....

    intent ....
....

Space to write, draw, scribble...

DATE ____/____/____

affirmation ....
....
   intent ....
....

Space to write, draw, scribble...

DATE ____/____/____

affirmation ....
....

   intent ....
....

Space to write, draw, scribble...

DATE ____ / ____ / ____

affirmation ....
....
    intent ....
....

Space to write, draw, scribble...

DATE ⌊_____/_____/_____⌋

affirmation ....
....

    intent ....
....

Space to write, draw, scribble...

DATE ___/___/___

affirmation ....
....

intent ....
....

Space to write, draw, scribble...

DATE ⌞_____/_____/_____⌟

affirmation ....
....

   intent ....
....

Space to write, draw, scribble...

DATE ⌞_____/_____/_____⌟

affirmation ....
....
   intent ....
....

Space to write, draw, scribble...

DATE ⌊_____/_____/_____⌋

affirmation ....
....

   intent ....
....

Space to write, draw, scribble...

DATE ⌞_____/_____/_____⌟

affirmation ....
....
    intent ....
....

Space to write, draw, scribble...

DATE ⌊_____/_____/_____⌋

affirmation ....
....

intent ....
....

Space to write, draw, scribble...

DATE ⌊_____/_____/_____⌋

affirmation ....
....
    intent ....
....

Space to write, draw, scribble...

DATE ____/____/____

affirmation ....
....

   intent ....
....

Space to write, draw, scribble...

DATE ⌊_____ / _____ / _____⌋

affirmation ....
....
     intent ....
....

Space to write, draw, scribble...

DATE ____/____/____

affirmation ....
....

   intent ....
....

Space to write, draw, scribble...

DATE _____/_____/_____

affirmation ....
....

intent ....
....

Space to write, draw, scribble...

DATE _____/_____/_____

affirmation ....
....

   intent ....
....

Space to write, draw, scribble...

DATE ____ / ____ / ____

affirmation ....
....
   intent ....
....

Space to write, draw, scribble...

DATE ⌊_____/_____/_____⌋

affirmation ....
....

    intent ....
....

🎁	_____
👁	_____
👂⭐	_____
🗺	_____
✋	_____
👄	_____
🧠	_____
❤️⚡	_____
☐	

Space to write, draw, scribble...

DATE ⌊_____/_____/_____⌋

affirmation ....
....
    intent ....
....

Space to write, draw, scribble...

DATE _____/_____/_____

affirmation ....
....

    intent ....
....

Space to write, draw, scribble...

DATE _____ / _____ / _____

affirmation ....
....

intent ....
....

Space to write, draw, scribble...

DATE ⌊_____/_____/_____⌋

affirmation ....
....

     intent ....
....

Space to write, draw, scribble...

DATE   /   /

affirmation ....
....
    intent ....
....

Space to write, draw, scribble...

DATE ⌊_____/_____/_____⌋

affirmation ....
....

   intent ....
....

Space to write, draw, scribble...

DATE ___/___/___

affirmation ....
....

intent ....
....

Space to write, draw, scribble...

DATE ⌊_____/_____/_____⌋

affirmation ....
....

    intent ....
....

Space to write, draw, scribble...

DATE ____/____/____

affirmation ....
....

   intent ....
....

Space to write, draw, scribble...

DATE ⌞_____/_____/_____⌟

affirmation ....

....

intent ....

....

Space to write, draw, scribble...

DATE ____/____/____

affirmation ....
....

intent ....
....

Space to write, draw, scribble...

Checking in

For the next few weeks, I intend to…

What I'm feeling now is…

I am aware that…

I am inspired by…

What motivates me is…

This month, I want to remember…

I wish…

Others are...

What matters most to me now is...

My strengths are...

My weaknesses are...

Things that annoy me are...

I hope that...

Reflecting on the past few weeks

A challenge I tackled recently...

The past few weeks looked like this...

The past few weeks sounded like this...

Last month started like this...

Last month ended like this...

My favourite moment of the past few weeks is...

This month I noticed...

This month I learned...

DATE _____/_____/_____

affirmation ....
....
      intent ....
....

Space to write, draw, scribble...

DATE ⌊_____/_____/_____⌋

affirmation ....
....
    intent ....
....

Space to write, draw, scribble...

DATE ____/____/____

affirmation ....
....

   intent ....
....

Space to write, draw, scribble...

DATE ⌊_____/_____/_____⌋

affirmation ....
....

   intent ....
....

Space to write, draw, scribble...

DATE ____/____/____

affirmation ....
....

   intent ....
....

Space to write, draw, scribble...

DATE _____ / _____ / _____

affirmation ....
....

intent ....
....

Space to write, draw, scribble...

DATE ___/___/___

affirmation ....
....

   intent ....
....

Space to write, draw, scribble...

DATE _____/_____/_____

affirmation ....
....

  intent ....
....

Space to write, draw, scribble...

DATE ___/___/___

affirmation ....
....

    intent ....
....

Space to write, draw, scribble...

DATE ____/____/____

affirmation ....
....
  intent ....
....

Space to write, draw, scribble...

DATE ____/____/____

affirmation ....
....

    intent ....
....

Space to write, draw, scribble...

DATE _____ / _____ / _____

affirmation ....
....

intent ....
....

Space to write, draw, scribble...

DATE ⌊⎯⎯⎯⎯⎯/⎯⎯⎯⎯⎯/⎯⎯⎯⎯⎯⌋

affirmation ....

....

    intent ....

....

Space to write, draw, scribble...

DATE ____/____/____

affirmation ....
....

intent ....
....

Space to write, draw, scribble...

DATE ⌊_____/_____/_____⌋

affirmation ....
....

    intent ....
....

Space to write, draw, scribble...

DATE   /   /

affirmation ....
....

    intent ....
....

Space to write, draw, scribble...

DATE ___/___/___

affirmation ....
....

   intent ....
....

Space to write, draw, scribble...

DATE _____/_____/_____

affirmation ....
....

    intent ....
....

Space to write, draw, scribble...

DATE ⌊_____/_____/_____⌋

affirmation ....
....

intent ....
....

Space to write, draw, scribble...

DATE ____ / ____ / ____

affirmation ....
....
   intent ....
....

Space to write, draw, scribble...

DATE _____/_____/_____

affirmation ....
....

   intent ....
....

Space to write, draw, scribble...

DATE ___/___/___

affirmation ....
....

intent ....
....

Space to write, draw, scribble...

DATE ___/___/___

affirmation ....
....

    intent ....
....

Space to write, draw, scribble...

DATE   /   /

affirmation ....
....

   intent ....
....

Space to write, draw, scribble...

DATE ___/___/___

affirmation ....
....

   intent ....
....

Space to write, draw, scribble...

DATE ⌊_____/_____/_____⌋

affirmation ....
....
   intent ....
....

Space to write, draw, scribble...

DATE ⌊_____/_____/_____⌋

affirmation ....
....

    intent ....
....

Space to write, draw, scribble...

DATE ___/___/___

affirmation ....
....

intent ....
....

Space to write, draw, scribble...

DATE ____/____/____

affirmation ....
....

   intent ....
....

Space to write, draw, scribble...

DATE ____/____/____

affirmation ....
....
    intent ....
....

Space to write, draw, scribble...

DATE   /   /

affirmation ....
....

   intent ....
....

Space to write, draw, scribble...

DATE ____/____/____

affirmation ....
....

   intent ....
....

Space to write, draw, scribble...

Checking in

For the next few weeks, I intend to...

What I'm feeling now is...

I am aware that...

I am inspired by...

What motivates me is...

This month, I want to remember...

I wish...

Others are...

What matters most to me now is...

My strengths are...

My weaknesses are...

Things that annoy me are...

I hope that...

Reflecting on the past few weeks

A challenge I tackled recently...

The past few weeks looked like this...

The past few weeks sounded like this...

Last month started like this...

Last month ended like this...

My favourite moment of the past few weeks is...

This month I noticed...

This month I learned...

DATE ____/____/____

affirmation ....
....

   intent ....
....

Space to write, draw, scribble...

DATE ___/___/___

affirmation ....
....

intent ....
....

Space to write, draw, scribble...

DATE ____/____/____

affirmation ....
....

    intent ....
....

Space to write, draw, scribble...

DATE ⌞_____/_____/_____⌟

affirmation ....
....

   intent ....
....

Space to write, draw, scribble...

DATE ___/___/___

affirmation ....
....

   intent ....
....

Space to write, draw, scribble...

DATE / /

affirmation ....
....

intent ....
....

Space to write, draw, scribble...

DATE ____/____/____

affirmation ....
....

    intent ....
....

Space to write, draw, scribble...

DATE ___/___/___

affirmation ....
....

intent ....
....

Space to write, draw, scribble...

DATE ___/___/___

affirmation ....
....

    intent ....
....

Space to write, draw, scribble...

DATE _____ / _____ / _____

affirmation ....
....

intent ....
....

Space to write, draw, scribble...

DATE ___/___/___

affirmation ....
....

   intent ....
....

Space to write, draw, scribble...

DATE ____/____/____

affirmation ....

....

intent ....

....

Space to write, draw, scribble...

DATE ___/___/___

affirmation ....
....

   intent ....
....

Space to write, draw, scribble...

DATE _____/_____/_____

affirmation ....
....

   intent ....
....

Space to write, draw, scribble...

DATE ___/___/___

affirmation ....
....

   intent ....
....

Space to write, draw, scribble...

DATE ⌊_____/_____/_____⌋

affirmation ....
....
  intent ....
....

Space to write, draw, scribble...

DATE ⌊_____/_____/_____⌋

affirmation ....
....

      intent ....
....

Space to write, draw, scribble...

DATE / /

affirmation ....
....
   intent ....
....

Space to write, draw, scribble...

DATE ⌞_____/_____/_____⌟

affirmation ....
....

  intent ....
....

Space to write, draw, scribble...

DATE ____/____/____

affirmation ....
....

intent ....
....

Space to write, draw, scribble...

DATE ⌊_____/_____/_____⌋

affirmation ....
....

   intent ....
....

Space to write, draw, scribble...

DATE ___/___/___

affirmation ....
....

   intent ....
....

Space to write, draw, scribble...

DATE ⌞_____/_____/_____⌟

affirmation ....
....

   intent ....
....

_____

_____

_____

_____

_____

_____

_____

_____

Space to write, draw, scribble...

DATE ⌊_____/_____/_____⌋

affirmation ....

....

  intent ....

....

Space to write, draw, scribble...

DATE ___/___/___

affirmation ....
....

   intent ....
....

Space to write, draw, scribble...

DATE ____/____/____

affirmation ....
....

   intent ....
....

Space to write, draw, scribble...

DATE ____/____/____

affirmation ....
....

intent ....
....

Space to write, draw, scribble...

DATE ___/___/___

affirmation ....
....

intent ....
....

Space to write, draw, scribble...

DATE   /   /

affirmation ....

....

     intent ....

....

Space to write, draw, scribble...

DATE _____ / _____ / _____

affirmation ....
....

intent ....
....

Space to write, draw, scribble...

DATE ___/___/___

affirmation ....
....

    intent ....
....

Space to write, draw, scribble...

DATE ___/___/___

affirmation ....
....

    intent ....
....

Space to write, draw, scribble...

Checking in

For the next few weeks, I intend to...

What I'm feeling now is...

I am aware that...

I am inspired by...

What motivates me is...

This month, I want to remember...

I wish...

Others are...

What matters most to me now is...

My strengths are...

My weaknesses are...

Things that annoy me are...

I hope that...

Reflecting on the past few weeks

A challenge I tackled recently...

The past few weeks looked like this...

The past few weeks sounded like this...

Last month started like this...

Last month ended like this...

My favourite moment of the past few weeks is...

This month I noticed...

This month I learned...

DATE ____/____/_____

affirmation ....
....

intent ....
....

Space to write, draw, scribble...

DATE ___/___/___

affirmation ....
....

intent ....
....

Space to write, draw, scribble...

DATE ___/___/___

affirmation ....
....

  intent ....
....

Space to write, draw, scribble...

DATE ⌊_____/_____/_____⌋

affirmation ....
....
    intent ....
....

Space to write, draw, scribble...

DATE ⌊_____/_____/_____⌋

affirmation ....
....

　　intent ....
....

Space to write, draw, scribble...

DATE   /   /

affirmation ....
....

   intent ....
....

Space to write, draw, scribble...

DATE ____/____/____

affirmation ....
....

   intent ....
....

Space to write, draw, scribble...

DATE   /   /

affirmation ....
....

intent ....
....

Space to write, draw, scribble...

DATE ⌊_____/_____/_____⌋

affirmation ....
....

   intent ....
....

Space to write, draw, scribble...

DATE ___/___/___

affirmation ....
....

intent ....

Space to write, draw, scribble...

DATE └────────/────────/────────┘

affirmation ....
....

   intent ....
....

Space to write, draw, scribble...

DATE   /   /

affirmation ....
....
   intent ....
....

Space to write, draw, scribble...

DATE _____/_____/_____

affirmation ....
....

    intent ....
....

Space to write, draw, scribble...

DATE ____/____/____

affirmation ....
....

intent ....
....

Space to write, draw, scribble...

DATE ⌞_____/_____/_____⌟

affirmation ....
....

 intent ....
....

Space to write, draw, scribble...

DATE ____/____/____

affirmation ....
....

intent ....
....

Space to write, draw, scribble...

DATE ___/___/___

affirmation ....
....

    intent ....
....

Space to write, draw, scribble...

DATE ⌊_____/_____/_____⌋

affirmation ....
....
intent ....
....

Space to write, draw, scribble...

DATE ..../........../..........

affirmation ....
....

intent ....
....

Space to write, draw, scribble...

DATE ____/____/____

affirmation ....
....
intent ....
....

Space to write, draw, scribble...

DATE ⌊_____/_____/_____⌋

affirmation ....
....

    intent ....
....

Space to write, draw, scribble...

DATE _____ / _____ / _____

affirmation ....
....

intent ....
....

Space to write, draw, scribble...

DATE ⌊_____/_____/_____⌋

affirmation ....
....

    intent ....
....

Space to write, draw, scribble...

DATE   /   /

affirmation ....
....

intent ....
....

Space to write, draw, scribble...

DATE _____ / _____ / _____

affirmation ....
....

intent ....
....

Space to write, draw, scribble...

DATE ____ / ____ / ____

affirmation ....
....

intent ....
....

Space to write, draw, scribble...

DATE ____/____/____

affirmation ....
....

    intent ....
....

Space to write, draw, scribble...

DATE ____/____/____

affirmation ....
....

intent ....
....

Space to write, draw, scribble...

DATE ⌊_____/_____/_____⌋

affirmation ....
....

　　　intent ....
....

Space to write, draw, scribble...

DATE ____/____/____

affirmation ....
....
   intent ....
....

Space to write, draw, scribble...

DATE ___/___/___

affirmation ....
....

   intent ....
....

Space to write, draw, scribble...

DATE ___/___/___

affirmation ....
....

intent ....
....

Space to write, draw, scribble...

Checking in

For the next few weeks, I intend to...

What I'm feeling now is...

I am aware that...

I am inspired by...

What motivates me is...

This month, I want to remember...

I wish...

Others are…

What matters most to me now is…

My strengths are…

My weaknesses are…

Things that annoy me are…

I hope that…

Reflecting on the past few weeks

A challenge I tackled recently...

The past few weeks looked like this...

The past few weeks sounded like this...

Last month started like this...

Last month ended like this...

My favourite moment of the past few weeks is...

This month I noticed...

This month I learned...

DATE ____/____/____

affirmation ....
....

   intent ....
....

Space to write, draw, scribble...

DATE   /   /

affirmation ....

....

   intent ....

....

Space to write, draw, scribble...

DATE ⌊_____/_____/_____⌋

affirmation ....
....

    intent ....
....

Space to write, draw, scribble...

DATE   /   /

affirmation ....
....
       intent ....
....

Space to write, draw, scribble...

DATE ___/___/___

affirmation ....
....

    intent ....
....

Space to write, draw, scribble...

DATE ___/___/___

affirmation ....
....
intent ....
....

Space to write, draw, scribble...

DATE ___/___/___

affirmation ....
....

   intent ....
....

Space to write, draw, scribble...

DATE ____/____/____

affirmation ....
....
    intent ....
....

Space to write, draw, scribble...

DATE ____/____/____

affirmation ....
....

  intent ....
....

Space to write, draw, scribble...

DATE   /   /

affirmation ....
....

   intent ....
....

Space to write, draw, scribble...

DATE ⌊＿＿＿＿／＿＿＿＿／＿＿＿＿⌋

affirmation ....
....

    intent ....
....

Space to write, draw, scribble...

DATE ____/____/____

affirmation ....
....

  intent ....
....

Space to write, draw, scribble...

DATE _____/_____/_____

affirmation ....
....

    intent ....
....

Space to write, draw, scribble...

DATE   /   /

affirmation ....
....

   intent ....
....

Space to write, draw, scribble...

DATE ____/____/____

affirmation ....
....

   intent ....
....

Space to write, draw, scribble...

DATE   /   /

affirmation ....
....

intent ....
....

Space to write, draw, scribble...

DATE ⌊_____/_____/_____⌋

affirmation ....
....

　　intent ....
....

Space to write, draw, scribble...

DATE ____/____/____

affirmation ....
....

intent ....
....

Space to write, draw, scribble...

DATE ___/___/___

affirmation ....
....

   intent ....
....

Space to write, draw, scribble...

DATE   /   /

affirmation ....
....
    intent ....
....

Space to write, draw, scribble...

DATE ⌊_____/_____/_____⌋

affirmation ....
....

    intent ....
....

Space to write, draw, scribble...

DATE   /   /

affirmation ....

....

intent ....

....

Space to write, draw, scribble...

DATE ⌞_____/_____/_____⌟

affirmation ....
....

    intent ....
....

Space to write, draw, scribble...

DATE   /   /

affirmation ....
....
        intent ....
....

Space to write, draw, scribble...

DATE ⌊_____/_____/_____⌋

affirmation ....
....

      intent ....
....

🎁	_____
👁	_____
👂	_____
🗺	_____
✋	_____
👅	_____
🧠	_____
❤️	_____
☐	

Space to write, draw, scribble...

DATE / /

affirmation ....
....
intent ....
....

Space to write, draw, scribble...

DATE ⌊_____/_____/_____⌋

affirmation ....
....

    intent ....
....

Space to write, draw, scribble...

DATE   /   /

affirmation ....
....
   intent ....
....

Space to write, draw, scribble...

DATE ⌊_____/_____/_____⌋

affirmation ....
....

    intent ....
....

Space to write, draw, scribble...

DATE ____/____/____

affirmation ....
....

intent ....
....

Space to write, draw, scribble...

DATE ⌊_____/_____/_____⌋

affirmation ....
....

   intent ....
....

Space to write, draw, scribble...

DATE ___/___/___

affirmation ....
....
intent ....
....

Space to write, draw, scribble...

Checking in

For the next few weeks, I intend to...

What I'm feeling now is...

I am aware that...

I am inspired by...

What motivates me is...

This month, I want to remember...

I wish...

Others are...

What matters most to me now is...

My strengths are...

My weaknesses are...

Things that annoy me are...

I hope that...

Reflecting on the past few weeks

A challenge I tackled recently...

The past few weeks looked like this...

The past few weeks sounded like this...

Last month started like this...

Last month ended like this...

My favourite moment of the past few weeks is...

This month I noticed...

This month I learned...

DATE ⌊_____/_____/_____⌋

affirmation ....
....

    intent ....
....

Space to write, draw, scribble...

DATE / /

affirmation ....
....

intent ....
....

Space to write, draw, scribble...

DATE ___/___/___

affirmation ....

....

  intent ....

....

Space to write, draw, scribble...

DATE / /

affirmation ....
....
   intent ....
....

Space to write, draw, scribble...

DATE ⌊_____/_____/_____⌋

affirmation ....
....

intent ....
....

Space to write, draw, scribble...

DATE   /   /

affirmation ....
....

    intent ....
....

Space to write, draw, scribble...

DATE ___/___/___

affirmation ....
....

intent ....
....

Space to write, draw, scribble...

DATE _____ / _____ / _____

affirmation ....

....

intent ....

....

Space to write, draw, scribble...

DATE ⌊_____/_____/_____⌋

affirmation ....
....

    intent ....
....

Space to write, draw, scribble...

DATE ___/___/___

affirmation ....
....

intent ....
....

Space to write, draw, scribble...

DATE ⌊_____/_____/_____⌋

affirmation ....
....

   intent ....
....

Space to write, draw, scribble...

DATE / /

affirmation ....
....
intent ....
....

Space to write, draw, scribble...

DATE _____/_____/_____

affirmation ....
....

   intent ....
....

Space to write, draw, scribble...

DATE __ / __ / __

affirmation ....

....

intent ....

....

Space to write, draw, scribble...

DATE ⌊_____/_____/_____⌋

affirmation ....
....

    intent ....
....

Space to write, draw, scribble...

DATE / /

affirmation ....

....

intent ....

....

Space to write, draw, scribble...

DATE ____/____/____

affirmation ....
....

    intent ....
....

Space to write, draw, scribble...

DATE _____/_____/_____

affirmation ....
....

intent ....
....

Space to write, draw, scribble...

DATE ____ / ____ / ____

affirmation ....
....

intent ....
....

Space to write, draw, scribble...

DATE ____/____/____

affirmation ....
....
  intent ....
....

Space to write, draw, scribble...

DATE ⌞_____/_____/_____⌟

affirmation ....
....

    intent ....
....

Space to write, draw, scribble...

DATE / /

affirmation ....
....
   intent ....
....

Space to write, draw, scribble...

DATE ⌊_____/_____/_____⌋

affirmation ....
....

   intent ....
....

Space to write, draw, scribble...

DATE _____/_____/_____

affirmation ....
....
        intent ....
....

Space to write, draw, scribble...

DATE ___/___/___

affirmation ....
....
   intent ....
....

Space to write, draw, scribble...

DATE   /   /

affirmation ....
....

intent ....
....

Space to write, draw, scribble...

DATE ⌊_____/_____/_____⌋

affirmation ....
....

    intent ....
....

Space to write, draw, scribble...

DATE   /   /

affirmation ....
....
       intent ....
....

Space to write, draw, scribble...

DATE ____/____/____

affirmation ....
....

   intent ....
....

Space to write, draw, scribble...

DATE   /   /

affirmation ....
....

intent ....
....

Space to write, draw, scribble...

DATE ⌞_____/_____/_____⌟

affirmation ....
....

    intent ....
....

Space to write, draw, scribble...

DATE / /

affirmation ....
....
  intent ....
....

Space to write, draw, scribble...

Checking in

For the next few weeks, I intend to…

What I'm feeling now is…

I am aware that…

I am inspired by…

What motivates me is…

This month, I want to remember…

I wish…

Others are...

What matters most to me now is...

My strengths are...

My weaknesses are...

Things that annoy me are...

I hope that...

Reflecting on the past few weeks

A challenge I tackled recently...

The past few weeks looked like this...

The past few weeks sounded like this...

Last month started like this...

Last month ended like this...

My favourite moment of the past few weeks is...

This month I noticed...

This month I learned...

DATE ___/___/___

affirmation ....
....

    intent ....
....

Space to write, draw, scribble...

DATE ____/____/____

affirmation ....
....
intent ....
....

Space to write, draw, scribble...

DATE ____/____/____

affirmation ....
....

   intent ....
....

Space to write, draw, scribble...

DATE ____/____/____

affirmation ....

....

 intent ....

....

Space to write, draw, scribble...

DATE ____/____/____

affirmation ....
....

    intent ....
....

Space to write, draw, scribble...

DATE   /   /

affirmation ....
....
     intent ....
....

Space to write, draw, scribble...

DATE   /   /

affirmation ....
....
        intent ....
....

Space to write, draw, scribble...

DATE _____/_____/_____

affirmation ....
....

intent ....
....

Space to write, draw, scribble...

DATE ⌊_____/_____/_____⌋

affirmation ....
....

      intent ....
....

Space to write, draw, scribble...

DATE   /   /

affirmation ....
....

   intent ....
....

Space to write, draw, scribble...

DATE ____/____/____

affirmation ....
....

intent ....
....

Space to write, draw, scribble...

DATE _____/_____/_____

affirmation ....
....

intent ....
....

Space to write, draw, scribble...

DATE ____ / ____ / ____

affirmation ....
....

intent ....
....

Space to write, draw, scribble...

DATE   /   /

affirmation ....
....

    intent ....
....

Space to write, draw, scribble...

DATE ___/___/___

affirmation ....
....

    intent ....
....

Space to write, draw, scribble...

DATE   /   /

affirmation ....
....
       intent ....

Space to write, draw, scribble...

DATE ____/____/____

affirmation ....
....

  intent ....
....

Space to write, draw, scribble...

DATE ⌞_____/_____/_____⌟

affirmation ....
....

intent ....
....

Space to write, draw, scribble...

DATE   /   /

affirmation ....
....

   intent ....
....

Space to write, draw, scribble...

DATE _____ / _____ / _____

affirmation ....
....

intent ....
....

Space to write, draw, scribble...

DATE ⌞_____/_____/_____⌟

affirmation ....
....

   intent ....
....

Space to write, draw, scribble...

DATE ___/___/___

affirmation ....
....
   intent ....

Space to write, draw, scribble...

DATE ____/____/____

affirmation ....
....

    intent ....
....

Space to write, draw, scribble...

DATE ___/___/___

affirmation ....
....

intent ....
....

Space to write, draw, scribble...

DATE ____/____/____

affirmation ....
....

intent ....
....

_____

_____

_____

_____

_____

_____

_____

_____

Space to write, draw, scribble...

DATE ____ / ____ / ____

affirmation ....
....

intent ....
....

Space to write, draw, scribble...

DATE ____/____/____

affirmation ....
....

   intent ....
....

Space to write, draw, scribble...

DATE ___/___/___

affirmation ....
....

intent ....
....

Space to write, draw, scribble...

DATE ⌊_____/_____/_____⌋

affirmation ....
....

    intent ....
....

Space to write, draw, scribble...

DATE   /   /

affirmation ....
....
    intent ....
....

Space to write, draw, scribble...

DATE ___/___/___

affirmation ....
....

intent ....
....

Space to write, draw, scribble...

DATE / /

affirmation ....
....
  intent ....
....

Space to write, draw, scribble...

Reflecting on your mindful journaling

How's it been for you?

Were you able to practice?

What helped you achieve your goal?

If you didn't, what stopped you?

What is your mindfulness practice? How would you describe it?

Are you able to be patient with yourself during your mindfulness practice?

How do you gently return to your focus as your mind drifts?

What insights have you gained from observing your mind?

What differences are there in your daily life that may have resulted in your mindfulness practice?

Have you noticed any changes in your professional life that might be due to your mindfulness practice?

Have your relationships and how you manage them changed as a result of your mindfulness practice?

If you'd like to continue your mindfulness journey,
there are more journals available on our publisher's website.
We have journals for adults and children:

Identitywithheld.com

We'd love to hear about your experiences of filling in this journal
— do drop us a line:

hello@identitywithheld.com

Also available

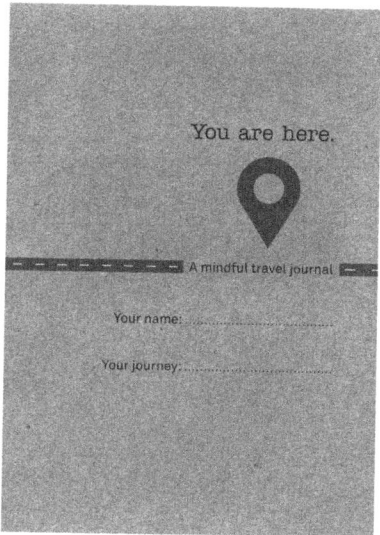

You are here. A mindful travel journal
By Emma Clarke

No-one has ever seen this place in the same way you're seeing it right now, right here, in this moment.

You Are Here is a travel journal that takes you on your own internal voyage of discovery. By using simple mindfulness techniques you'll find ways to develop a happy, peaceful mind.

Many people buy a beautiful notebook to take on holiday. For some, the emptiness of all those pages is daunting. You Are Here guides you through a rich variety of exercises designed to help you thoroughly enjoy your gap year, city break, odyssey, holiday-of-a-lifetime, 'find yourself' journey or weekend away. You'll use fresh, creative thinking to save a memory on every page.

Every moment is precious. Every moment is unique. Use this journal to live each moment to the max.

ISBN 978-1-910306-00-0

"Sit. Breathe. Love. is an imprint of Identity Withheld Ltd."

Available at identitywithheld.com, Amazon and all good bookshops.

Sit. Breathe. Love is proud to support the charity
VillagebyVillage.org.uk
If you'd like to donate to Village by Village, just click:
www.sitbreathelove.com/donate

Village by Village – Who We Are

Village by Village was established in 2006 after the founder witnessed the implication of a lack of clean water, sanitation and education in remote disadvantaged rural communities in Ghana. The charity was established to respond to the needs of these communities by supporting the reduction of poverty and needless hygiene-related deaths through the provision of simple but powerful resources and opportunities.

Since 2006 projects established have provided toilets, clean drinking water, scholarship programmes to enable children to attend school and support for individuals to start up their own businesses. The charity has grown to a team of 10 dedicated staff, nine of whom are based in country. We work in partnership with those people living in poverty in the rural villages as we have found this provides the greatest impact. Through this way of working, Ghanaian based project contractors and volunteers have established solid partnerships and so work in collaboration to best deliver the projects, adding value to the work of others operating in Ghana.

Impact to Date

Our original aim was to reach 100 villages by 2016 with sanitation, clean drinking water education for children and business skills. We were able to reach this aim by February 2012 four years ahead of schedule due to the effectiveness of the partnership working with community members in the villages in Ghana which included the incorporation of community ideas and knowledge and the employment and engagement of those within the communities.

Through our work we have supported approximately 35,000 people in 100 villages to reduce poverty and to improve their self-sustainability, health and life chances. Since 2006 we have delivered:

- Completed 36 toilet projects in communities and schools to help reduce deaths due to poor sanitation

- 4 wells built to provide clean drinking water in villages

- 2 rain water harvesting projects for hand washing projects in schools in communities in poverty

- 711 children provided with the opportunity to educate their way out of poverty through the provision of scholarships

- 6 businesses developed to support sustainable incomes

- A health clinic was built in Gboloo, Kofi which has been staffed by the local health service

- A school library and information centre was established to provide information on health, hygiene, sanitation and family planning to the remote villages surrounding Gboloo, Kofi

- Built a crèche and kindergarten allowing very young children to access a village school

- Built a Junior High School in the remote rural village of Gboloo Kofi

- Built a Primary School block and computer lab in the remote rural village of Abenta

The Need – Preventable Death

Having spent six years working alongside communities in poverty working together to provide sanitation projects Village by Village have found the biggest impact in saving the lives of children and reducing pain and suffering amongst families does not simply come from providing toilets and wells, but must be combined with teaching the importance of washing hands with soap.

Diarrhoeal disease remains one of the world's biggest killers, with UNICEF estimating it kills a child every 30 seconds. In Ghana, diarrhoea accounts for 25 percent of all deaths in children under five and is among the top three reported causes of deaths.

While hand-washing in the UK may help prevent a stomach bug, in poorer countries it is the most effective and in-expensive way to save lives. Without ready access to hand washing facilities including running water and soap, coupled with an understanding of its importance, entire communities will remain at risk. Turning hand washing with soap before and after eating and using the toilet into an ingrained habit could save more lives than any single vaccine or medical intervention, cutting deaths from diarrhoea by almost half and deaths from acute respiratory infections by one-quarter.

Village by Village have witnessed the impact of poor sanitation first hand though our 100 Village's project. This project offered toilets and hand washing facilities to households and communities as a whole.

It is now our priority to establish the importance of sanitation throughout those communities we have worked in, to ensure further lives are not unnecessarily lost.

The Solution – Clean Hands Saves Lives, an integrated approach

To improve the life chances of some of the most vulnerable individuals and communities within Ghana our 'Clean Hands Saves Lives' project will provide sanitation facilities whilst also addressing behavioural change to support a life-time impact.

During 2012-16 we will target 5,600 children aged 6-16 with the facilities, resources and education to ingrain the washing of hands following toilet use. Children are strategically being targeted to provide the greatest impact as not only do they suffer disproportionally from diarrhoeal diseases, it has been proven that once children change their behaviour, 80 percent are then likely to pass their learning to their own families.

To ensure the necessary change takes place to improve health and life chances, the project will be implemented within two separate phases:

1. **Providing the tools**

   Each project will begin with the help of our local and international volunteers who work alongside our team of Ghanaian builders to build a three toilet block within a school. These toilet blocks support sanitation as their self composting design ensures flies entering the toilet are trapped inside the pit latrine. Their larvae develop into maggots which eat away the faeces.

   Polytanks (plastic water tanks) and guttering is used to collect rainwater that will support hand washing. With the use of a veronica bucket (a plastic container designed with a tap at the bottom) water is released into a bowl acting as a sink. All equipment can be locally replaced and repaired to increase the longevity of the project. Soap will be provided by the school as a sign of their commitment before a school is selected.

2. **Behaviour Change**

Once the necessary tools have been provided, an intensive supporting phase will commence over a 18 month period. This will establish new patterns of behaviour to embed hand-washing to improve sanitation. The Ghana Health Service and the Education Service will join the project at this stage, providing teachers and nurses to talk to the local school children alongside headteachers who will engage village Chiefs and Elders who will support the community wide message and enhance commitment to the project. We provide the teachers and children with promotional materials to incentive, reward and encourage behaviour change, including t-shirts, stickers, posters and baseball caps.

Once the community is engaged, the children will be targeted through a 'Bog Watch' initiative. This will act as an engagement tool with volunteers recruited as behavioural change agents. As recommended by the local headteachers consulted, a rota system will be put into place to encourage hand-washing with classmates acting as hand-washing monitors. Teams of school children will be tasked with designing and brightly painting the toilet blocks and water tanks with promotional hand-washing messages aimed at their classmates.

To further enhance commitment to the project, children and members of the local community will be chosen as 'star' actors to appear in a hand washing flash-mob film. This is screened as a whole community movie-night using a projector and a white sheet. This creates an exciting and memorable experience for the community as a whole as such events are very rarely held. An example of a film made can be found via: **www.villagebyvillage.org.uk**

Monitoring and Evaluation

We will put in place a comprehensive monitoring and evaluation system to measure the impact of the project. This will include the following:

- A baseline survey with regular surveys thereafter recording the outputs and the impact of the project.

The following will also be implemented as an engagement opportunity, however the data collected will also be used within the monitoring process over the 18 month period:

- Playground surveys conducted by the children
- Child centric and adult centric 'bog watch' carried out by school children / members of the community assessing the number of people washing their hands following visits to the toilet.

How to donate

With your support we hope to continue to make a difference to some of the poorest communities in Ghana, improving health and saving lives.

To donate to Village by Village, just click:
www.sitbreathelove.com/donate

Lightning Source UK Ltd.
Milton Keynes UK
UKOW07f0359271114

242258UK00009B/143/P